SNAKES

by GAIL GIBBONS

Holiday House / New York

To Kate Briggs

Special thanks to
Bill Holmstrom, herpetologist
at the Bronx Zoo, Bronx, New York

HOLIDAY HOUSE is registered in the U.S. Patent and Trademark Office.
Printed and bound in January 2012 at Worzalla, Stevens Point, WI, USA.
www.holidayhouse.com
5 7 9 10 8 6 4

Library of Congress Cataloging-in-Publication Data
Gibbons, Gail.
Snakes / by Gail Gibbons. — 1st ed.
p. cm.
ISBN-13: 978-0-8234-2122-0 (hardcover)
1. Snakes—Juvenile literature. I. Title.
QL666.O6G33 2007
597.96—dc22
2007024585
ISBN 978-0-8234-2300-2 (paperback)

Blades of grass sway back and forth in a meadow. Something silently and slowly slithers as it moves forward. It is a snake.

Ancient Egyptians believed snakes had the power to determine life and death.

In ancient Mexico people believed snakes were gods.

Ancient Greeks used snakes as a symbol of healing. A snake's image wrapped around a staff stood for good health and a long life.

Native American Hopi Indians still perform a snake dance to ask the gods for rain.

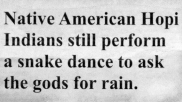

Today, a symbol of healing is two snakes wrapped around a staff. It is called a caduceus (kah·DO·sus).

Snakes have existed for about 125 million years. Throughout history some people have believed snakes have special powers. Ancient cultures expressed their beliefs in the powers they thought snakes held. They showed this in what they did, what they wore, and what they passed down through legends and myths.

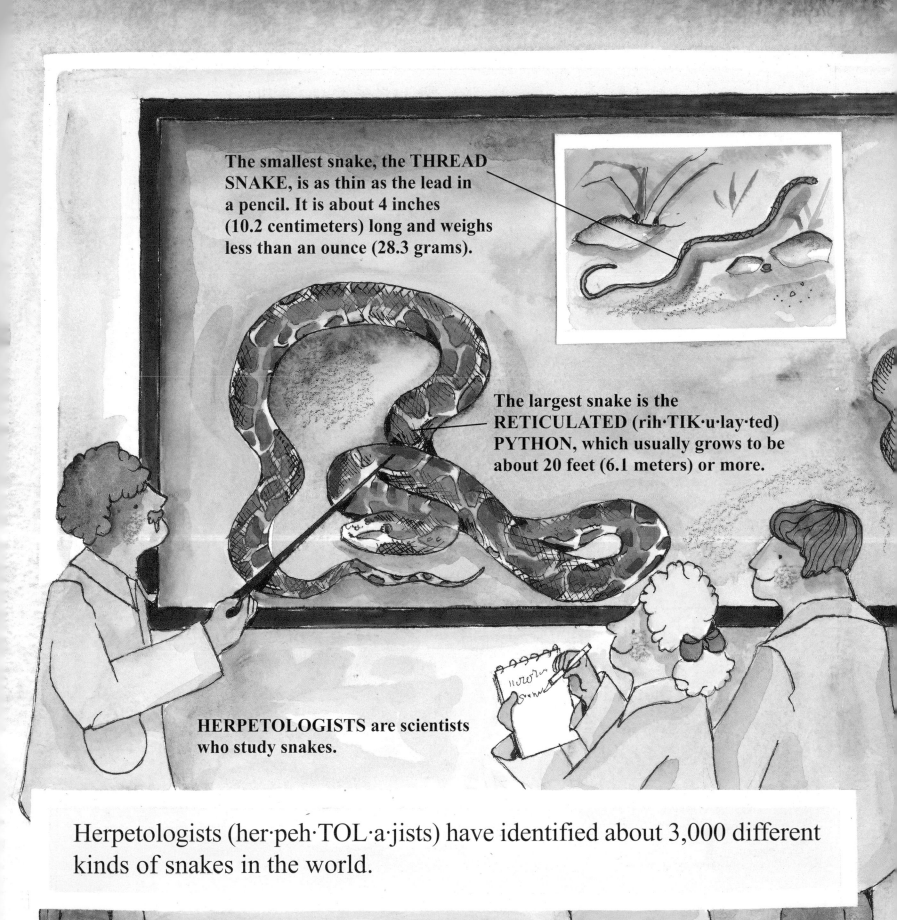

The smallest snake, the THREAD SNAKE, is as thin as the lead in a pencil. It is about 4 inches (10.2 centimeters) long and weighs less than an ounce (28.3 grams).

The largest snake is the RETICULATED (rih·TIK·u·lay·ted) PYTHON, which usually grows to be about 20 feet (6.1 meters) or more.

HERPETOLOGISTS are scientists who study snakes.

Herpetologists (her·peh·TOL·a·jists) have identified about 3,000 different kinds of snakes in the world.

WHERE SNAKES LIVE

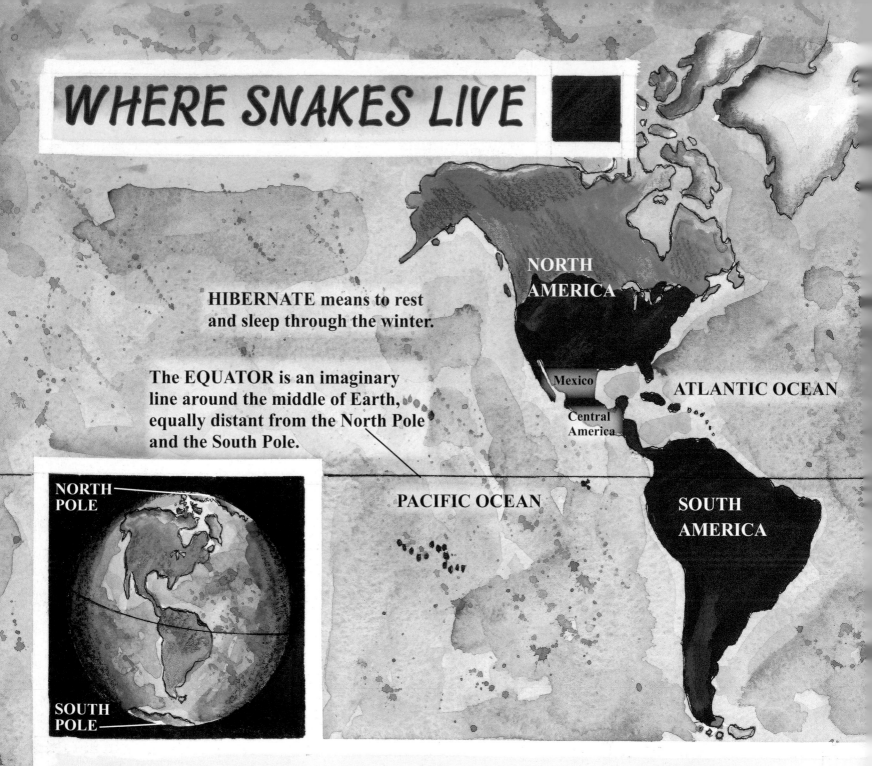

HIBERNATE means to rest and sleep through the winter.

The EQUATOR is an imaginary line around the middle of Earth, equally distant from the North Pole and the South Pole.

NORTH POLE

SOUTH POLE

NORTH AMERICA

Mexico

Central America

ATLANTIC OCEAN

PACIFIC OCEAN

SOUTH AMERICA

Snakes live throughout most of the world. Most kinds of snakes live in warm climates near the equator, where it is warm enough to survive. In colder climates snakes hibernate underground through the winter months so they won't freeze.

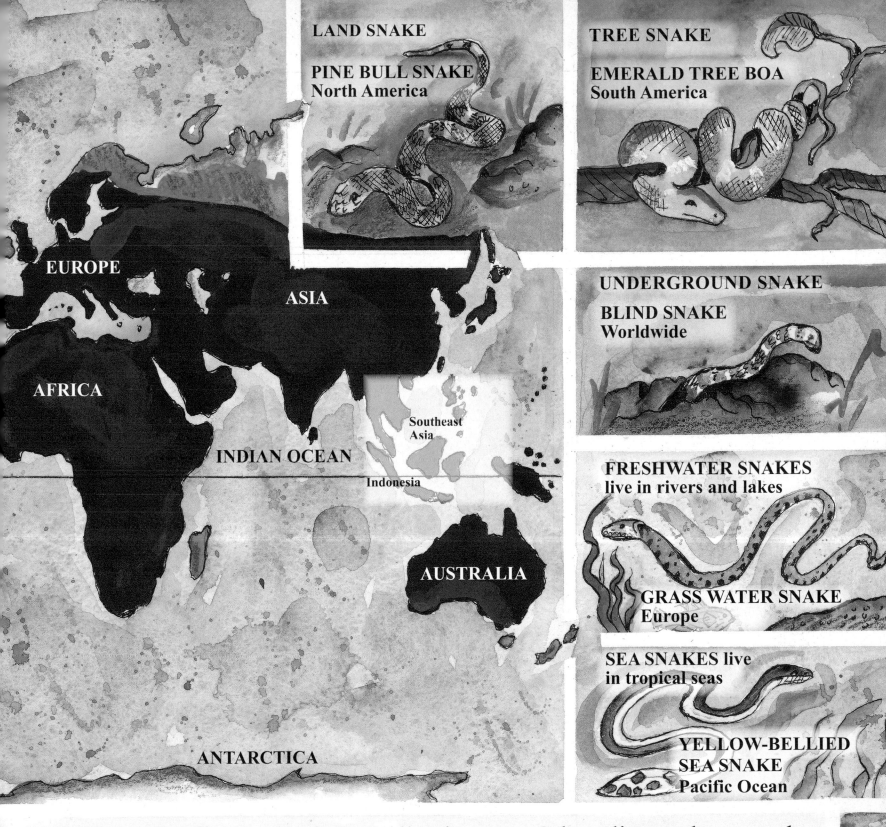

LAND SNAKE

PINE BULL SNAKE
North America

TREE SNAKE

EMERALD TREE BOA
South America

UNDERGROUND SNAKE

BLIND SNAKE
Worldwide

EUROPE

ASIA

AFRICA

Southeast
Asia

INDIAN OCEAN

Indonesia

AUSTRALIA

ANTARCTICA

FRESHWATER SNAKES
live in rivers and lakes

GRASS WATER SNAKE
Europe

**SEA SNAKES live
in tropical seas**

**YELLOW-BELLIED
SEA SNAKE**
Pacific Ocean

Most snakes live on land. Some live in trees. Others live underground, and still others live in water.

A SNAKE'S BODY

SPECTACLES are transparent scales that protect the eyes. Snakes have no eyelids, so they can't close their eyes.

The NOSTRILS are used for breathing and smelling.

INNER EARS

HEAD

BODY

TEETH

JAW

Their SCALES are part of their skin.

A FORK-SHAPED TONGUE helps test for scents.

FANGS

VENOMOUS

Snakes are reptiles. Unlike other reptiles, such as turtles, lizards and alligators, snakes have no arms or legs. Their skins are dry and flexible, and have scales. Some snakes have fangs.

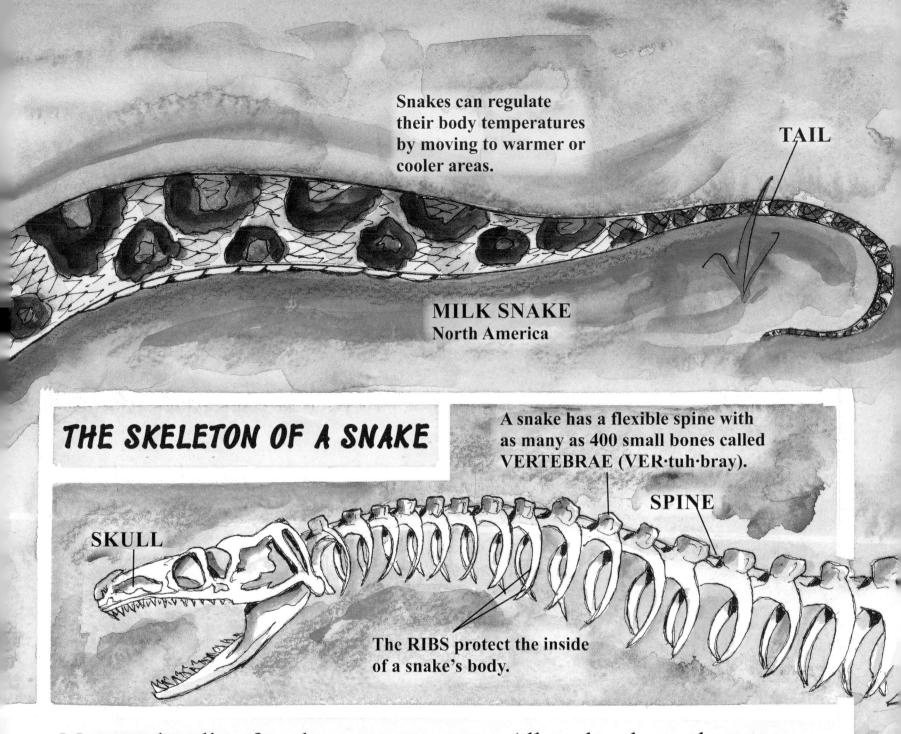

Snakes can regulate their body temperatures by moving to warmer or cooler areas.

TAIL

MILK SNAKE
North America

THE SKELETON OF A SNAKE

A snake has a flexible spine with as many as 400 small bones called VERTEBRAE (VER·tuh·bray).

SPINE

SKULL

The RIBS protect the inside of a snake's body.

Most snakes live for about twenty years. All snakes have the same basic characteristics. However, the shapes of their heads, bodies, and tails can vary, as well as the colors and patterns of their skins. That's because the many kinds of snakes have different ways of hunting for food and finding protection.

HOW SNAKES MOVE

RETICULATED PYTHON
Southeast Asia

COMMON CORAL SNAKE
North America

Snakes use their strong body muscles to move in different ways. Many snakes move forward in a straight line by gripping the ground as they go. Others bunch their bodies together, straighten them out and then pull themselves forward. This is called bunching.

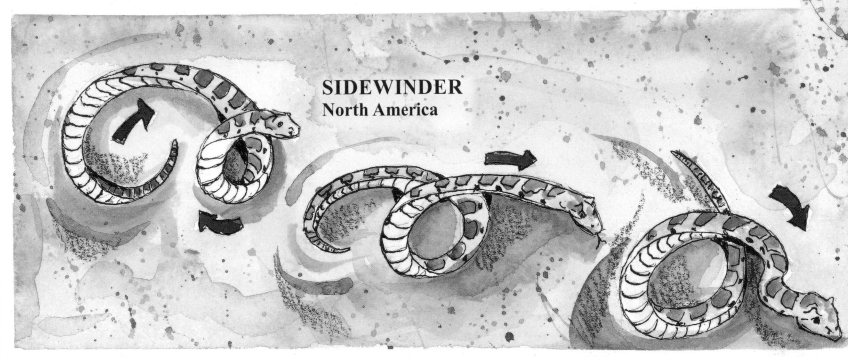

SIDEWINDER
North America

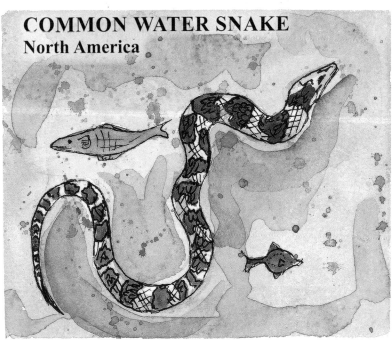

COMMON WATER SNAKE
North America

BANDED SEA SNAKE
Pacific Ocean

Some snakes move by throwing and looping their bodies forward over and over again. Freshwater snakes and sea snakes use their muscles to wiggle from side to side in order to glide through the water. Sea snakes have paddle-shaped tails to help them swim.

HOW SNAKES GET THEIR FOOD

EASTERN KING SNAKE
North America

Snakes are carnivores. That means they only feed on other animals. They only attack when hungry.

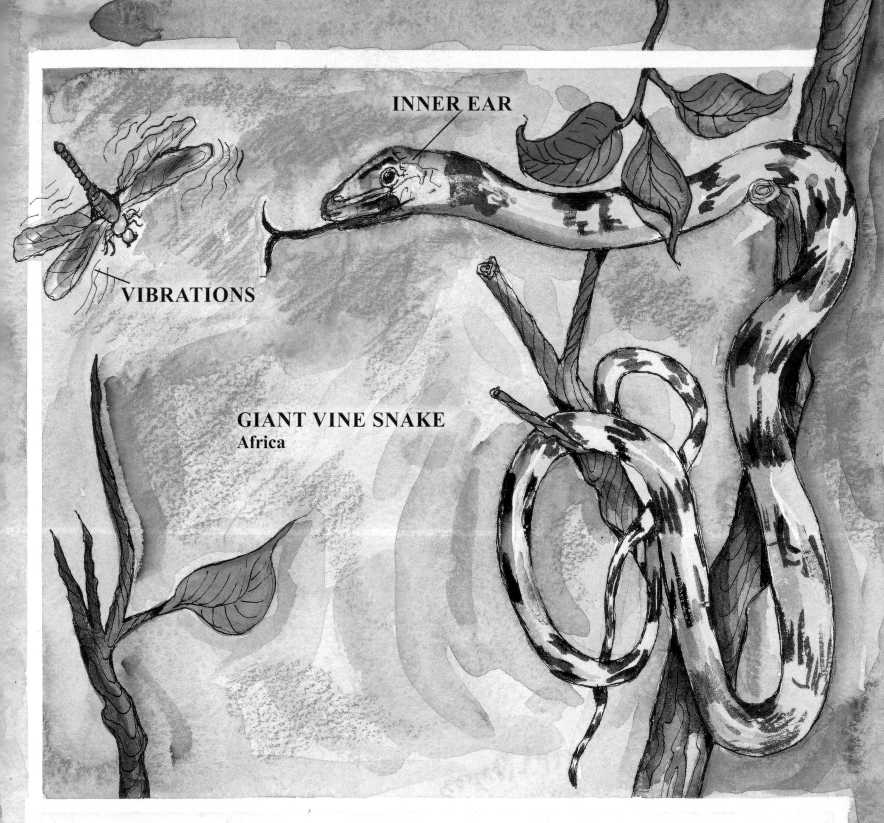

INNER EAR

VIBRATIONS

GIANT VINE SNAKE
Africa

Snakes do not have outer ears, but they do have inner ear structures that can pick up vibrations.

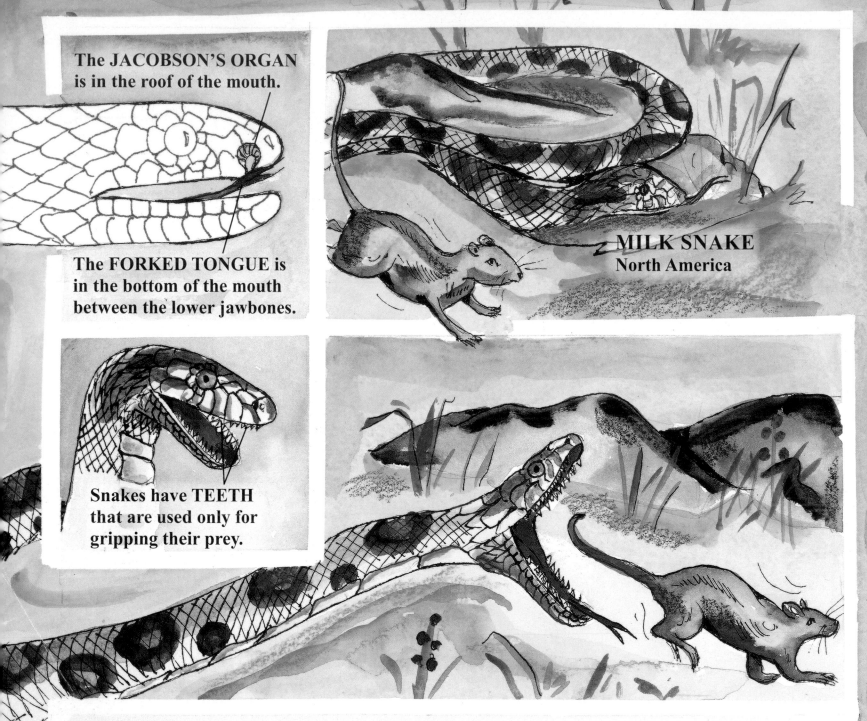

The **JACOBSON'S ORGAN** is in the roof of the mouth.

The **FORKED TONGUE** is in the bottom of the mouth between the lower jawbones.

Snakes have **TEETH** that are used only for gripping their prey.

MILK SNAKE
North America

The snake uses its flicking forked tongue to pick up scents. Then when the tip of the tongue touches the Jacobson's organ, the snake is able to identify what it is smelling. If it is food, the snake stays very still and then suddenly attacks.

A SNAKE'S JAW

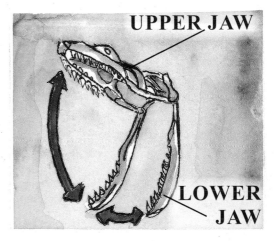
UPPER JAW

LOWER JAW

All snakes swallow their prey whole. Some kill their prey first. Others do not. A snake can swallow an animal much larger than its own head because its rigid jawbones are loosely connected and thus its jaw can expand. The snake's body also expands as it takes in its prey.

SOME COMMON SNAKES

SAN FRANCISCO GARTER SNAKE
North America

BLIND SNAKE
Worldwide

EASTERN GARTER SNAKE
North America

SMOOTH GREEN SNAKE
North America

KING SNAKE
North America

NORTHERN BLACK RACER
North America

These snakes are harmless to humans.

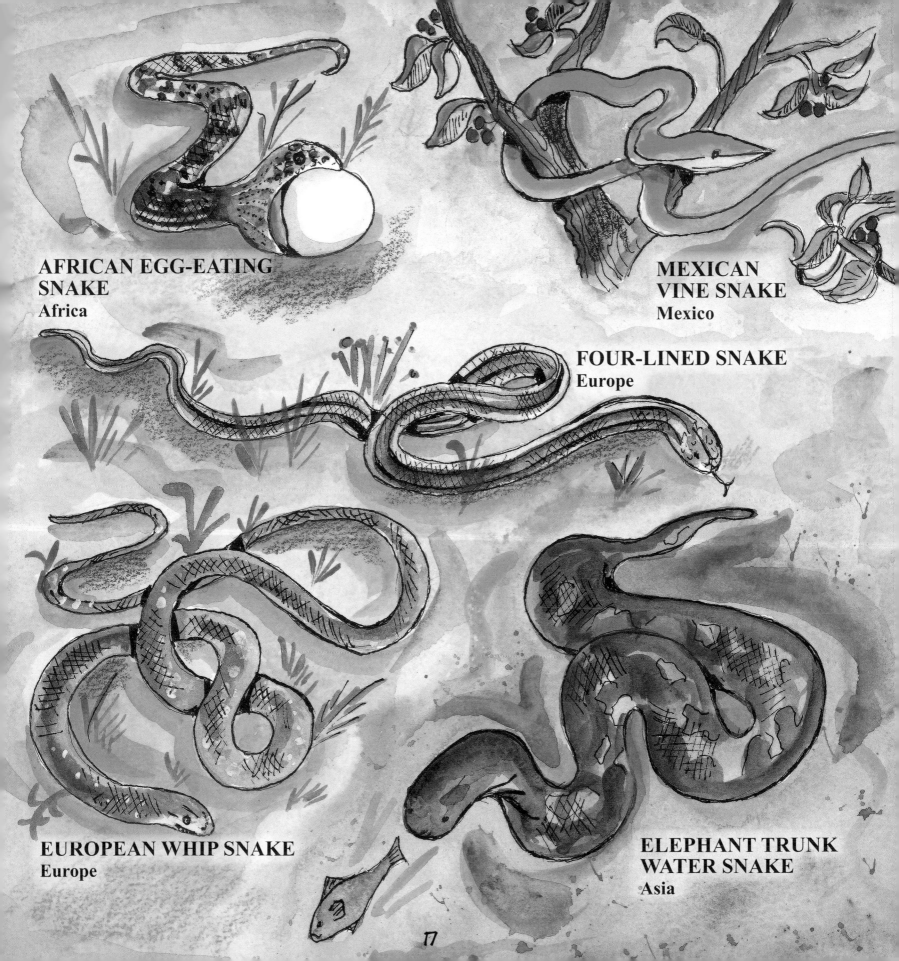

AFRICAN EGG-EATING SNAKE
Africa

MEXICAN VINE SNAKE
Mexico

FOUR-LINED SNAKE
Europe

EUROPEAN WHIP SNAKE
Europe

ELEPHANT TRUNK WATER SNAKE
Asia

SOME VENOMOUS SNAKES

SONORAN CORAL SNAKE
North America

SIDEWINDER
North America

TIGER RATTLESNAKE
Australia

VENOMOUS FANGS

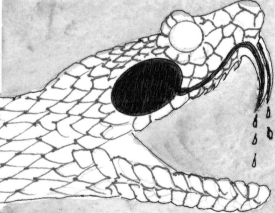

The FANGS are the two longer, hollow teeth that appear either at the front or the back of the mouth.

A snake injects VENOM from a SAC into its prey through needle-sharp hollow FANGS.

WESTERN DIAMONDBACK RATTLESNAKE
North America

EASTERN DIAMONDBACK RATTLESNAKE
North America

BOOMSLANG
Africa

These snakes use their venom to stun or kill prey before swallowing them.

FER-DE-LANCE
Central America

BUSHMASTER
Central and
South America

SPECTACLED COBRA
Southeast Asia

BLACK MAMBA
Africa

KING COBRA
Southeast Asia

There are about 250 species of venomous snakes.

SOME CONSTRICTOR SNAKES

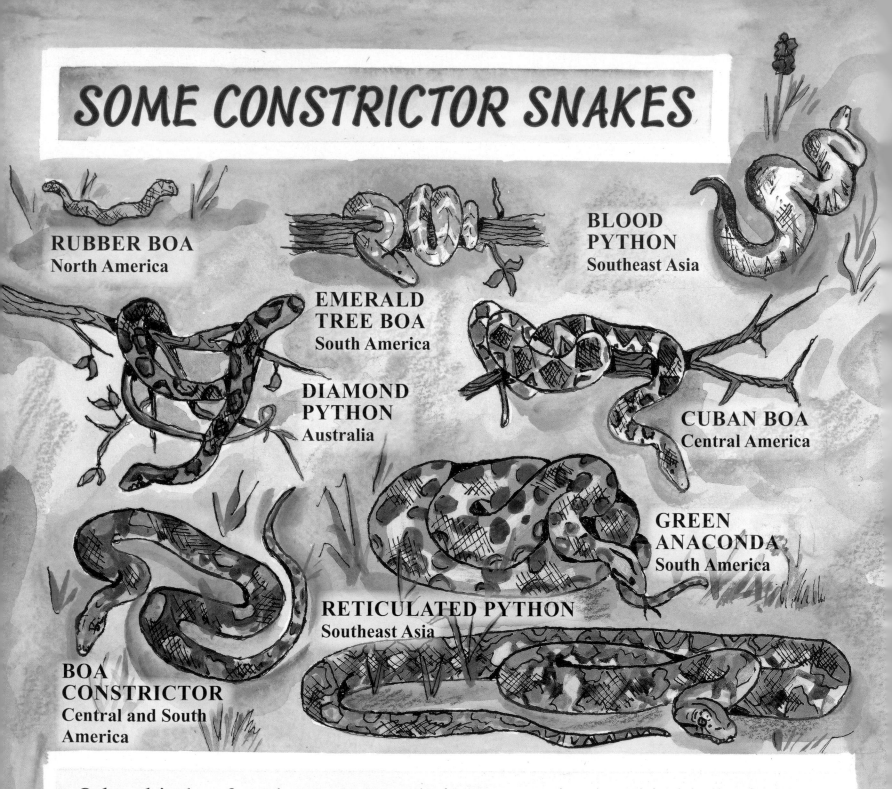

RUBBER BOA
North America

EMERALD TREE BOA
South America

BLOOD PYTHON
Southeast Asia

DIAMOND PYTHON
Australia

CUBAN BOA
Central America

GREEN ANACONDA
South America

RETICULATED PYTHON
Southeast Asia

BOA CONSTRICTOR
Central and South America

Other kinds of snakes squeeze their prey to death. This kind of snake is called a constrictor because the word *constrict* means "to squeeze." There are more than 150 kinds of constrictor snakes.

DIAMOND PYTHON
Australia

The snake attacks its victim by grabbing it with its teeth. Then it wraps its body around its prey in tight coils. Once its catch stops breathing, the snake expands its jaws to swallow its prey.

Some snakes blend in with their backgrounds. This is called CAMOUFLAGE (KAH·muh·flaaj). It helps them avoid being discovered by their enemies.

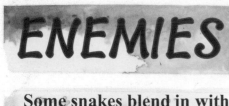

SIDEWINDER
North America

Others PUFF UP to look bigger and make hissing sounds as a warning.

PUFF ADDER
Africa

Some snakes have rattles at the ends of their tails that they RATTLE as warnings.

WESTERN DIAMONDBACK RATTLESNAKE
North America

Some snakes spread the loose skin around their heads to make HOODS. This makes them look bigger.

KING COBRA
Southeast Asia

Some snakes show very BRIGHT COLORS to startle attackers.

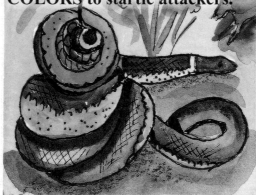

RINGNECK SNAKE
North America

HOGNOSE SNAKE
North America

Other snakes do a number of things, such as HISSING, PUFFING themselves up, SPREADING their HOODS. If these fail, they PLAY DEAD.

Snakes have enemies. They can be birds or other animals and sometimes people. Most of the time snakes are not aggressive. If they sense danger, they try to avoid it. Usually they try to slither away as fast as possible. If they can't escape, snakes use different ways to defend themselves.

SPITTING COBRA
Africa

Some snakes SPIT VENOM into the face of their enemies to temporarily blind them.

MONGOOSE

SECRETARY BIRD

MONGOOSE

In a fight for their own survival, most snakes will bite their enemies over and over again.

Different kinds of snakes lay from two to one hundred eggs.

COMMON CORAL SNAKE
North America

A female python will coil herself around her eggs to help keep them warm. The eggs will hatch in about eighty days.

RETICULATED PYTHON
Southeast Asia

The EGG TOOTH will drop off when a young snake sheds its first skin.

EGG TOOTH

HATCHLING SNAKE

Usually snakes mate once a year. Most snakes lay eggs. Two or three months after mating, the eggs are laid in a warm place and are usually left unattended. When the snakes are ready to hatch, they each use a special sharp egg tooth to slit open their leathery shells. Now they are hatchlings and are able to live on their own right away.

RAINBOW BOA
South America

CASINGS, also
called SACS

Some snakes give birth to live young about seven months after mating. Before being born, the snakes are in casings, which are also called sacs. They leave their sacs almost immediately after they are born. These snakes are also able to live on their own right away.

A snake usually sheds its skin several times in its first year because it is growing so quickly. Older snakes shed their skin about once a year.

LEAF-NOSED SNAKE
North America

OLD SKIN

When it is time, the snake will separate itself from its old skin and leave it behind. They can do this in a few minutes.

Snakes never stop growing. The bodies of young snakes grow very quickly, but their skins do not. They must shed the outer layer of old skin. The skin underneath becomes the new outer layer. Each time their bodies outgrow their skin they shed their skin again.

DEN

EASTERN GARTER SNAKES
North America

Snakes may use dens to sleep in and to protect them from bad weather. In colder climates snakes hibernate during the winter so they won't freeze to death. Some hibernate alone. Others hibernate in groups. When spring arrives, they will become active again.

HOW PEOPLE ENDANGER SNAKES

EASTERN GARTER SNAKES
North America

SMOOTH GREEN SNAKE
North America

NORTHERN BLACK RACER
North America

Today there are fewer snakes living in their natural environments. People have moved into areas in which snakes once lived. Land is cleared. Trees are cut down to make lumber. There are fewer places where snakes and other wildlife can live.

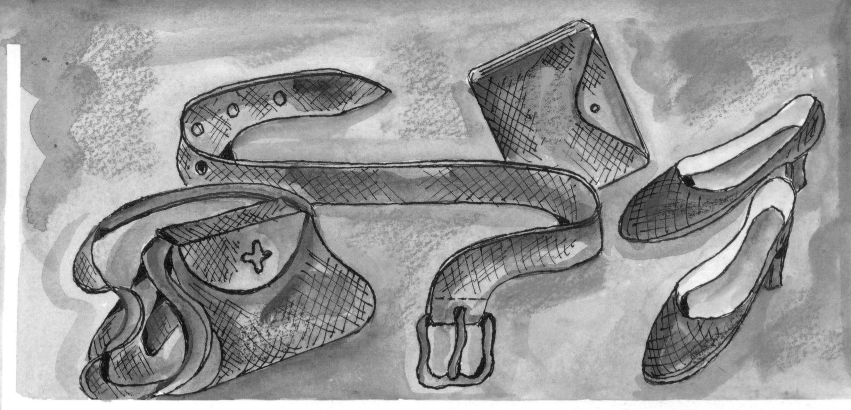

BLACK RAT SNAKE
North America

EASTERN GARTER SNAKE
North America

TRANS-PECOS COPPERHEAD
North America

Some people hunt snakes for their beautiful skins. The skins are used to make items such as belts, purses, and shoes. Some people kill snakes because they are afraid of them. Most snakes arc harmless.

BLACK-AND-WHITE COBRA
Africa

WILDLIFE PRESERVE

BOOMSLANG
Africa

GREEN MAMBA
Africa

EXTINCT means to no longer exist.

There are wildlife preserves where snakes are safe from people. Some zoos have learned ways to care for and keep endangered snakes from becoming extinct.

Like all animals, snakes play a role in the balance of nature. To know about snakes is to admire and respect them. They are fascinating animals.

SLITHERING SNAKES

Usually female snakes are larger than males.

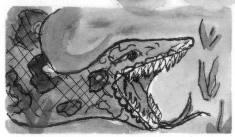
Some snakes, such as pythons, have two rows of teeth in the front of the upper jaw.

Garter snakes are the most widespread snakes in North America.

The oldest known snake lived for about forty-seven years. It was a ball python that was kept at the Philadelphia Zoo.

The western diamondback rattlesnake is usually about 4 feet (1.22 meters) long.

Snakes do not exist in nature in New Zealand, Ireland, Iceland, or Antarctica.

The eastern diamondback rattlesnake is the longest venomous snake in North America, usually about 5 feet (1.52 meters) long.

If you see a snake in the wild **DO NOT GO NEAR IT!**

Snakes are wild animals and should be allowed to live in their natural habitat.

Some snakes that live in trees can flatten their bodies and glide through the air from one branch to a lower branch or to the ground.

HELP! IF YOU ARE EVER BITTEN BY A SNAKE, TELL AN ADULT IMMEDIATELY.